Nick Birch

Using humour in advertising effectively

GRIN Verlag

Bibliografische Information der Deutschen Nationalbibliothek:

Die Deutsche Bibliothek verzeichnet diese Publikation in der Deutschen National-
bibliografie; detaillierte bibliografische Daten sind im Internet über http://dnb.d-
nb.de/ abrufbar.

Imprint:

Copyright © 2011 GRIN Verlag GmbH
Druck und Bindung: Books on Demand GmbH, Norderstedt Germany
ISBN: 978-3-656-60880-6

This book at GRIN:

http://www.grin.com/en/e-book/269678/using-humour-in-advertising-effectively

GRIN - Your knowledge has value

Der GRIN Verlag publiziert seit 1998 wissenschaftliche Arbeiten von Studenten, Hochschullehrern und anderen Akademikern als eBook und gedrucktes Buch. Die Verlagswebsite www.grin.com ist die ideale Plattform zur Veröffentlichung von Hausarbeiten, Abschlussarbeiten, wissenschaftlichen Aufsätzen, Dissertationen und Fachbüchern.

Visit us on the internet:

http://www.grin.com/

http://www.facebook.com/grincom

http://www.twitter.com/grin_com

USING HUMOUR IN ADVERTISING EFFECTIVELY

Nick Birch 2011

"Humour is the great thing, the saving thing. The minute it crops up, all our irritation and resentments slip away, and a sunny spirit takes their place." - Mark Twain

INTRODUCTION

Advertising is all about getting attention. One of the best ways of getting attention through advertising is adding humour. When employed correctly, the power of humour is undeniable. Professional Advertising (N/A) believes that '[t]he best ways to get attention with advertising are with strong visuals, sex, powerful headlines, and humour.'

From all the types of advertising appeals, such as *Emotional, Rational, Sex, Scarcity* and *Humour*, '[h]umour can be an excellent tool to catch the viewer's attention and help in achieving instant recall which can work well for the sale of the product. Humour can be used effectively when it is related to some benefit that the customer can derive without which the joke might overpower the message' (Ashwini, 2009). Humour is most effective when it is used to reinforce an existing message, rather than simply adding to it.

Catanescu & Tom (2001) maintain that '[a]s previous research has revealed... [their] study shows that humour is used more frequently in television commercials than print advertisements' and so it is with this acumen that generates the focus on television commercials. What humour achieves exactly can differ from one advertiser to the next, but its primary function seems to be about getting attention, regardless if it is good or bad attention.

According to a 1993 Journal of Marketing study that examined multinational effects of humour on advertising, 'humour is more likely to enhance recall, evaluation, and purchase intention when the humorous message coincides with ad objectives, is well-integrated with those objectives, and is viewed as appropriate for the product category. Under such circumstances, humorous advertising is more likely to secure audience attention, increase memorability, overcome sales resistance, and enhance message persuasiveness' (Dubois, 2010).

TYPES OF HUMOUR

Professional Advertising (N/A) warns that 'humour is in the eye of the beholder. It is commonly misinterpreted. Many people [may] not get the joke'. In order to acquire a more tactile understanding of how humour is used effectively in advertising, it may be beneficial to recognize some of the different types of humour.

Catanescu & Tom (2001) outline several different types of humour;

- Comparison
- Personification
- Exaggeration
- Pun/Parody
- Sarcasm
- Silliness
- Surprise

To illustrate how some of these types of humour can be used effectively, let us first examine three beer commercials from three different brands.

The grandiose, operatic performance in Carlton Draught's *Big Ad* seen in Slide 2 is an example of *exaggeration* bordering on *silliness,* through which the advertiser achieves a somewhat self-depreciating humour, 'which is safer than making fun of someone else who may be offended, which can cause you to lose a customer' (Richardson, 2011). By poking fun at themselves and what they do, the advertiser can show that they understand the viewer's cynicism for traditional advertising methods used to promote products and how cliché and repetitive they can be.

The smooth and sexy bulk of Hahn's *Venice* commercial is also a parody of traditional advertising methods, in this instance using sex to sell. In Slide 3 we are caught off-guard when the man lands a fish all over his sensuous female companion. In this example of *surprise* humour, the advertiser may also be exaggerating the boisterous nature of the man depicted in the commercial to improve the product's image, which is essentially a light beer and may not be considered "manly" by their target consumer. This is solidified by the slogan "some drink it because they're responsible", a pun alluding to responsible drinking which also highlights the advertiser's safety message. This contrast combined with the element of surprise results in an effective use of humour which is directly related to the product.

It is important to be product-specific when using humour in advertising. Smith warns us 'not to use humour for its own sake' as '[o]ften it so happens that people get so indulged in a funny advertisement that they almost forget or ignore the product or service being advertised'. Along with the temptation to use humour, an advertiser must take care to 'ensure that the humour is very directly related to [their] business' (Smith, N/A). Humour should be used in advertising only if it is relevant to the advertiser's objective. Professional Advertising (N/A) concurs that '[a]dvertising humour must relate directly to your business or products if you want to be remembered. And advertising humour has a relatively short life. The first time we see it we may laugh out loud. But after a while, although we still may smile at the joke, it's not so funny anymore'.

Heineken's *Walk-in Fridge* commercial is a good example of maximising the life of the type of humour used. In Slide 4 we clearly see the use of *comparison* when the reactions of the two sexes are portrayed. As the couple show off their new home to friends, the women shriek in delight upon seeing the large walk-in wardrobe, only to be outdone by the exaggerated squealing of the men upon discovering the walk-in fridge full of beer. The use of *exaggeration* and *silliness* are also used somewhat in the achievement of this humour. Even though the joke may get old, watching the men's overstated excitement seems timeless. By keeping in mind that humour has a short life, the advertiser has used a combination of types of humour to increase the life of the ad. 'A joke which appears to be funny when heard or viewed for the first time gradually loses the interest of the audience' (Smith, N/A) but in this case the life of the humour lives on when competing brands parody the joke.

Bavaria spoofs the Heineken *Walk-in Fridge* commercial in Slide 5 and adds the element of a Bavaria-drinking man trumping the Heineken men and thus stealing the joke. Whether Bavaria parodies in a competitive nature, it still seems to be a bow to the effectiveness of the joke, appropriating the idiom from Charles Caleb Colton - "imitation is the sincerest of flattery" (Quote DB, N/A). The advertisers of Heineken could not ask for a better result than their competition enhancing the life of their commercial at their own cost.

Sometimes parodies can help a product enter the minds of a completely different target audience. The well-known Old Spice commercial in Slide 6 has been spoofed time and time again in many ways. Interestingly, in Slide 7 *Sesame Street* has their turn annexing their own twists to advertise the program, using their special brand of child-like *silliness* along the way. Nothing is child-like about the "toy" featured in Slide 8, however.

IKEA endeavours to be product-specific with their special brand of naughty European humour in their commercial *Tidy Up!* This humour may fall under the heading of *comparison*, if one is to compare the two very different kinds of toys that the child is playing with. The horror and *surprise* of the realisation seems a very valid reason to indeed "tidy up" – and there IKEA is with their product solutions. This commercial may be seen as riskier than the others due to its potentially offensive nature, though airing times and cultural influences may play a part in its reception and success. It is certainly a risk since IKEA is such as large company and may not profit from risk-taking as much as a smaller company might. Humour may be credited in attaining attention for an advertisement and fostering a positive attitude for a product, but as Catanescu & Tom (2001) question, '[o]n the other hand, the use of humour may not be suitable for certain products or services, is thought to lead to faster advertising "wear out", may offend some members of the audience and may result in the so-called "vampire effect," where the humour sucks attention away from the advertised product/message'. There is also the risk that others (depending on the audience) simply may not understand what the starring item in IKEA's commercial is.

> 'Advertising humour also needs to be well suited to its audience. If your customers
> don't get the joke, then the joke will be on you. A sophisticated audience will
> understand your irony, satire, and puns, but a young audience may only understand
> slapstick comedy or a silly cartoon caricature. Inside jokes can be effective if the
> recipient understands that it was done for them, but nobody else will get it. And
> advertising humour can backfire. If you make a joke at the expense of any one group,
> you will surely alienate them.' (Professional Advertising, N/A)

Using humour in advertising can backfire when it becomes offensive to a certain group, but it may not be as reputation-damaging as repeatedly using weak humour.

INEFFECTIVE HUMOUR IN ADVERTISING

Using humour in advertising can work for or against the objective of its use. Effective humour draws people to the message advertisers are attempting to convey:

> *'It keeps the attention of your prospect. It makes your message easier to remember. It's more likely they'll tell others about your advertising. It tells others that you and your company have a sense of humour. On the other hand, be careful with humour in advertising. Weak humour can undermine your credibility. It can detract from your advertising message. A frequently appearing ad with weak humour can often be a big turnoff to potential customers. It can reflect negatively on your judgment.' (Kinde, 2005)*

Privately owned Australian family business *Titan Garages & Sheds* have a long-running and on-going television campaign (Titan Garages, N/A) that may be perceived as using weak humour. Over time, the father and son team seem to now portray themselves as some kind of pseudo-celebrities, moving further and further away from the original premise of advertising their product through cheesy attempts at comedy. In Fig.9, the latest addition to this saga can be seen as an example of a smaller company using humour to perhaps compete with larger companies. 'The great thing for smaller companies is that with humour, you can compete with the goliaths [as consumers] don't care how big your company is or what your budget was. If it's funny and good, that's what matters' (Washer, N/A). The weak humour used in the Titan commercials runs the risk of detracting from the advertiser's message and their product may be better served by adding more product information instead. Although Titan's humour may or may not be effective in advertising their product, they do seem to be somewhat memorable, an achievement which is at least one of the main reasons for using humour in advertising.

As Creative Director of *Morey Evans Advertising*, Tom Evans remarks:

> *'It's kind of like trying to jump over the net after a tennis match. If you make it, you're golden. If you don't, you're gonna catch a foot and flip on your head and look like an idiot (funny as that may be).'* (Evans, N/A)

CONCLUSION

Some pervasive traits of the types of humour used in the selected effective commercials are that they memorable, remain related to the product and use simple jokes with longevity.

Humour in advertising is risky, but as Professional Advertising (N/A) claims, when done right 'it can also be devastatingly effective'. Attempting to pinpoint what makes something funny is near impossible. Humour certainly is in the eye of the beholder, but what makes that humour effective in advertising is whether or not that sense of humour is shared by the target audience.

> *Is there something logical about why everyone seems to respond to humour? No! That's the point. People respond to humour with their emotions, not with their reason, so as a marketer you can slip past their left-brained defences and launch a guerrilla assault on where they really live and experience life. Don't over-analyse a humorous idea. It's funny, or it's not. As Mark Twain said, "Trying to figure out why something is funny is like dissecting a frog. You'll come up with answers, but the frog always dies."* (Stroh, N/A)

REFERENCES

Ambekar, Ashwini. (2009). *Different Types of Advertising Appeals.* Available:

http://www.articleswave.com/advertising-articles/types-of-advertising-appeals.html. Last

accessed 12th March 2011.

Catanescu, Codruta; Tom, Gail. (2001). *Types of Humour in Television and Magazine*

Advertising. Available: http://www.entrepreneur.com/tradejournals/article/76941382.html.

Last accessed 22nd March 2011.

Dubois, Lou. (2010). *How to Use Humour in Advertising.* Available:

http://www.inc.com/guides/2010/12/how-to-use-humor-in-advertising.html. Last accessed

20th March 2011.

Evans, Tom. (N/A). *Why Be Funny in Radio?.* Available: http://www.ad-mkt-

review.com/public_html/docs/fs060.html. Last accessed 20th March 2011.

Kinde, John. (2005). *Using Humour in Advertising.* Available: http://www.clown-

ministry.com/index_1.php/articles/using_humor_in_advertising/. Last accessed 12th March

2011.

Professional Advertising. (N/A). *Laugh Out Loud - Advertising Humour.* Available:

http://www.myprofessionaladvertising.com/Humor%20in%20Advertising.htm. Last accessed

22nd March 2011.

Quote DB. (N/A). *Charles Caleb Colton.* Available: http://www.quotedb.com/quotes/810. Last

accessed 26th March 2011.

Richardson, Tim. (2011). *Kewl Commercials / Weird Ads.* Available:

http://www.witiger.com/marketing/kewlcommercials-weirdads.htm. Last accessed 26th

March 2011.

Smith, Susan. (N/A). *Bringing Humour in Your Online Business Advertisements Effectively.*

Available: http://www.affordable-internet-marketing.com/2011/01/online-business-

advertisements/. Last accessed 12th March 2011.

Stroh, Don. (N/A). *The Serious Side of Humour in Direct Marketing.* Available: http://www.ad-mkt-review.com/public_html/docs/fs060.html. Last accessed 20th March 2011.

Titan Garages. (N/A). *Titan TV.* Available: http://www.titangarages.com.au/titan-tv/. Last accessed 26th March 2011.

Washer, Tim. (N/A). *How to Use Humour in Advertising.* Available: http://www.inc.com/guides/2010/12/how-to-use-humor-in-advertising_pagen_2.html. Last accessed 26th March 2011.